LAUNCH TO MARKET

EASY MARKETING FOR AUTHORS

CHRIS FOX

To Indies. Do this writing thing, and stand proud.

CONTENTS

WRITE FASTER, WRITE SMARTER SERIES

5,000 Words Per Hour
Lifelong Writing Habit
Write to Market
Launch to Market
Six Figure Author
Relaunch Your Novel

INTRODUCTION

If you are anything like me you hate long introductions. I don't care about the author's trophies, and I don't need a lengthy overview of what I'm about to learn. Just tell me what problem you're going to solve, and then teach me how to do it.

You're about to learn a set of marketing tools that will help you launch (or re-launch) your book in a way that will help it sell. Some of these tools require capital, either money or time. Selling books in today's digital world is difficult. It requires work, patience, diligence, and most importantly testing.

Before you buy Launch to Market, ask yourself the following tough questions. Are you willing to do a brutal self-assessment, and then do the work required to take your author business to the next level? If the answer to both questions is yes, then by all means click that buy button so I can purchase my next cup of coffee.

Wait a minute, though. The tagline for this book is EASY marketing for authors. Brutal self-assessment doesn't sound easy.

There's a huge difference between *easy* and *effortless*. If you want your sales to improve you'll need to implement the steps given throughout the book. It contains exercises, and the book is only valuable if you do them. If you're not ready to do them at the time you read them, that's okay. I've gathered them into a chapter at the end, so you can do them after finishing if you prefer.

It doesn't matter so much *when* you do them, just that you do them. If you're not willing, I'd suggest saving yourself three bucks and not purchasing this book. It won't be useful.

Why Should You Listen to Me?

Because I sell a LOT of books.

When you use titles like *5,000 Words Per Hour* and *Write to Market* you tend to attract a lot of skeptics. Many people claimed that it was impossible to write as quickly as I do, and that even if you *could*, whatever you produced would be crap. This despite the fact that I'm not the first, or even the hundredth writer to crank out books this quickly.

In February of 2016 I very publicly tested the methods I teach in this series. I wrote and edited my novel *Destroyer* in 21 days, and I documented the entire thing on video (you can watch those at chrisfoxwrites.com). What's more, I boldly proclaimed that I could launch that book into the Amazon top #1,000, and that it would stay in the top #10,000 for the first 30 days.

I knew I could write the book in the time I'd allotted, but I had no idea how it would sell. If Destroyer flopped it would have crushed my credibility in the author community, and the chances of you buying this book would be nil. I put my money where my mouth is. I described exactly what I hoped to achieve, and then documented every tactic, step, and setback. I wanted to prove that I knew what I was talking about in a way that skeptics couldn't pick apart.

Spoilers, Destroyer sailed up to #198 in the entire store, selling 542 copies its first day. It stayed in the top #1,000 for the entire first month, and the book paid for its $2,300 in production costs within the first five days.

Launch to Market shows you everything I did, and more importantly explains *why* I did it. Not every tactic worked, and I'll talk about my failures as well. I encourage you to adopt the principles, not the tactics. By that, I mean you should adapt this material to your own launch. Don't just use it wholesale.

Okay, enough of the intro crap. Let's launch your book.

1

DESTROYER CASE STUDY

Before we dive into the meat of launching your book, I want to take a minute to talk about the novel *Destroyer*. It's referenced throughout this book, and for good reason. *Launch to Market* wouldn't exist without *Destroyer*.

So how are they linked? As I mentioned briefly in the intro, I wrote *Destroyer* publicly, using the principles I teach in the *Write Faster, Write Smarter* series. Its success was linked to the validity of my methods. If it failed, then I'd failed. If it succeeded, I had real proof that my system works.

Either way, I planned to take the exact same action. I would study the crap out of every facet of *Destroyer*'s launch, and then I'd optimize my process based on what I learned. That's exactly what I ended up doing, and here are some key take aways.

The Challenge

In February of 2016 I released a book called *Write to Market*. In that book, I explained that new authors can make a living writing in genres where they know there are a ton of readers. Whatever genre you picked, it still needed to be one that you loved.

In my case, I chose space opera. I love science fiction. Love. It. So writing about giant spaceships, my house cats thinly disguised as aliens, and brain eating slugs wasn't much of a stretch. Unfortunately, the people who disagreed with this methodology often ignored the second part. They assume that you need to write romance or erotica if you want to make the big dollars. You need to, in their words, sell your soul.

I published *Destroyer* to prove them wrong. I wanted to show that I could publish a book in a brand new genre where I had no fans, but still achieve success by writing a good book I knew readers would love.

I'm already known as the '*5,000 Words Per Hour* Guy', so I figured why not add a time limit? 21 days sounded good, so I pledged to write and edit the book in that time frame. People thought it sounded insane, but for me it was just the continuation of a process I'd been refining for three years. I knew I could write and edit a good book in three weeks. But would it sell?

That was the real question. I pledged to film daily videos for the writing process, then record the launch. I made good on both those promises, and you can see those video series at chrisfoxwrites.com, or on YouTube. The *Launch to Market* videos will be extremely useful, as they show how I implemented everything you're about to learn.

Sales Data

Fortunately for me, my system worked. *Destroyer* landed around #200 in the Amazon store on release day, selling over 500 copies. I kept it on sale for 99 cents for the first five days, then killed the sale early when the book settled in around #400 rank. Raising the price pushed the settling point down to about #700 in the entire store.

Destroyer is still around there at the time of this writing. It's sold 5,500 copies, and had a million pages read. That means the book earned 5 figures in its very first month, and I expect similar performance for the sequel.

I wrote *Destroyer* to market, and the market loves it. The book has a 4.6 star average with 97 reviews after only 30 days.

Where Are the Videos?

You'll find the videos tracking the launch of Destroyer at chrisfoxwrites.com/challenge. They're free, and I'd encourage you to use them as a companion resource. I won't keep linking them, as I know many of you are reading on Kindles and don't want to hassle with video. Just know that they're there, and that if things are not clear in the book you may find more help in the videos.

The Dangers of Fast Publishing

My favorite part of the challenge were the things I learned the hard way. Those lessons will stick with me forever, because I've rarely been that embarrassed.

After receiving the book back from my line

editor I realized that it needed a better ending. So I wrote a new epilogue chapter, and added it to the manuscript. No editor saw that chapter, and surprise, surprise...there was a huge error as a result. Every instance of the POV character's name was changed to another character.

This was extremely jarring to readers, as it knocked them out of the story. The error is mentioned in at least a half dozen reviews. I received over 50 emails about it. I corrected the book immediately, of course, but that didn't change the fact that thousands of people had the erroneous version.

So why am I telling this story? For two reasons. First, I want it clear that there is a cost to rapid publishing, and I paid that cost. Second, your audience will probably forgive you. Mistakes happen, but as long as you keep striving to improve that's all that matters. Do your best to release an excellent book, but don't get caught in the trap of trying to make it perfect.

Your launch will have some speed bumps. Accept that, learn from them, then launch the next book.

Mining Reviews

In *Write to Market* I talked a lot about how you can mine reviews for information about your target reader. This is critical during your launch, and here's my takeaways from *Destroyer*.

My readers like fast paced, sparsely detailed, action packed books. There are a flurry of 5 stars from people who absolutely loved the book, because it was a fast read. They mentioned that I didn't waste time explaining all the little details of how the science worked. I used it as dressing for the story.

The one star reviews (and there are several) say almost exactly the opposite. They wanted better description, and more accurate science. They hated the book, and thought it was trash. It didn't meet their expectations of a great SF novel.

So what's the take away here? That I wrote Destroyer exactly as intended. Its target audience loves it, and I'm not trying to cater to those expecting a different book. I might tighten my science up a little in future books, but only a little. More likely, I'll keep writing exactly like I'm writing. Almost 90% of people who read the book gave it a 4 or 5 star.

Why Was the Book So Successful?

We'll examine this throughout the book, but here's the short version. I figured out which books *Destroyer* was like, and then got it in front of the readers who liked those books. I knew that fans of Joshua Dalzelle, Nick Webb, M.R. Forbes, and other SF authors would love *Destroyer*. So I used targeted ads, word of mouth, networking, keywords, and categories to get my book in front of their readers.

It worked smashingly well, because Amazon now knows that people who bought from those authors will also buy *Destroyer*. That means they're doing the heavy lifting. My preparation was the match, but the gasoline is Amazon's algorithms.

By the end of the book you'll see exactly what I mean by that, and how you can apply the same lessons to your own books.

2

EVERYBODY STARTS AT 0

Before we get started on launching your book you need to set some realistic expectations. The success of your launch will be largely dependent upon the size of your platform. If you have 10,000 mailing list subscribers, 40,000 Twitter followers, and a 10 book backlist your launch will be quite a bit different from someone putting out their first novel.

To that end, this chapter begins the self-assessment I mentioned in the intro. Where are you in your author journey? There is no wrong answer. If you're only selling a handful of copies, that's totally okay. We're about to change that, but change takes time. You don't go from 0 to a million in a single step.

Everybody Starts at 0

When I began self-publishing I didn't have a mailing list. I'd never sold a copy of a book. I still remember my first sale and my first subscriber. They were both me. I remember wondering how I was going to get 10 people to sign up. It seemed impossible. Selling a thousand books seemed even more out of reach.

We all start at that level. If that's you, if you are picking this book up having never published a novel, that's totally okay. The numbers you hear may be daunting, but I'd encourage you to remember that you don't need to duplicate them immediately.

Every novel you write is another brick in your self-publishing fortress. Each time you place one, do it deliberately. Use the lessons you learned from previous launches to make this one better. Then make the one after that better.

There is no magic bullet. There is no 'one weird trick' to sell a million copies. Publishing is a hard business, but it has a set of understandable rules. These are rules you can master, and this book will teach you the fundamentals.

The core of the entire system is incremental improvement.

The Three Questions

The path to longterm success in this business is incremental self-improvement. Part of that self-improvement is mastering the ability not to compare yourself with other authors. Doing so used to make me feel inadequate and worthless. How the hell was I going to do what Hugh Howey just did? Or come anywhere even close?

I see this comparison-itis every day. Sometimes it's me that's guilty of it, and sometimes other authors. It's hard not to go there, but there are three questions that can free you from it.

1. Where were you yesterday?
2. Where are you today?
3. Where do you want to be tomorrow?

All you need to do is measure your own progress. Are you selling more books today? Do you have more mailing list subscribers? A bigger back list? Then you're kicking ass.

What if you're selling less? That's okay too. It's just a data point on your author graph. Tomorrow is another chance, and if you approach your career that way it feels much less daunting.

Focus on incremental improvement, and you'll get there.

One Thing a Day

So how does one go about this incremental improvement? You do one thing every single day to move toward your success. That single action can be tiny, but if you do another action every day they'll begin to compound. You will get momentum, which is a powerful, powerful force. If you harness it for a year, you'll barely recognize your author career at the end of it.

Incremental improvement offers one other tremendous advantage. It allows you to stop focusing on the big picture. You're no longer looking at your whole author career. You're not even looking at the success of a single book. You're just doing one action that will help both. If that action succeeds, awesome. If it fails, you learned something. Tomorrow, you'll take another action.

Maybe that's brainstorming marketing ideas with a couple author friends. Maybe it's booking your first Kindle Countdown Deal. Maybe you want to do a crazy YouTube challenge like I did. The specific action is up to you, but as long as you try something every day you'll guarantee you're closer than you were yesterday.

Finding Your Tier

Amazon book ranks are the key to understanding how well you're doing. The lower the rank, the better you're selling. Below you'll find a brief explanation of the tiers, and as you read them you'll figure out where you currently lie. The goal of this book is to teach you to advance one tier. If your book is currently ranked at Tier VI, can you get the next launch down to Tier V? If you're in five, can you get to four?

Tier VI- #100,000 to #999,999

You don't sell a book every day, but you're moving some each month.

Tier V- #10,000 - #99,999

You generally sell at least a book a day. If you're close to the #10,000 mark you're probably selling closer to 10 copies a day, and have some pages read if you're in Kindle Unlimited.

Tier IV- #1,000 - #9,999

This is where the real money starts to happen. At #9,999 you're selling double digits every day. By the time you get down to #1,000 you're selling around a hundred copies a day, or having thousands of page reads and double digit sales.

Tier III- #100 - #999

This is the highest I've ever gone, and the place where *Destroyer* landed after its recent release. At the #100 rank you are probably selling 1000+ copies a day, and have something like 100,000 page reads. This is where your titles begin earning five figures a month by themselves.

Tier II- #10 - 99

This is as high as most indies will ever see, and generally it only happens when we've launched a BookBub or some other massively discounted sale.

At this tier individual books could be earning *mid five figures* every month.

Tier I- #1-9

I can't even wrap my brain around this tier. If you plant a book in the top 10 odds are very high that you'll earn six figures a month from just that book.

Okay, now that we've looked at the scale, where do you lie? What rank is your best (or only) book at? Our goal will be to get your launch to break into the next tier. If you're at Tier VI, that's great news. Breaking into Tier V is much easier than Tier III.

Over time, books will slide down the tiers. Your Tier IV book will fall into Tier V between 60-90 days after release, in most cases. This is partly why pushing to the next tier is so important. If you can get your book into Tier III, then you'll be making great profit for months. By the time it slips to Tier IV, you'll be close to putting out the next book (or have already done so).

∾

Exercise #1- Set a reminder on your phone for the marketing action you're going to take tomorrow. How will you improve? Maybe it's reading this book. Commit to that action. Make sure it gets done.

Bonus: Repeat this process every day for the next week. At the end of the week measure where you are, versus where you were when you started. What did you accomplish?

Bonus II: Write down your best Tier.

3

EASY MARKETING

About the subtitle on the cover, the whole easy marketing thing? Yeah I was lying about that. Marketing isn't easy. It's *simple*.

Understanding what to do is easy. Taking the actions necessary to build your brand is much more difficult. That requires daily work, and before we go further I'm asking you one final time to commit to that work. If you're willing to do that, I can provide a *simple* system for launching, one that will help you craft a sustainable career.

Ready? Let's do this.

What Is Marketing?

The very word marketing transforms most writers into the proverbial deer in headlights. We work so hard on craft, toiling for months or years on our first novel. Then we finish it, and suddenly learn we need an entire different set of skills if we'd like to actually sell the thing.

Fortunately, marketing is way easier than I'd assumed when I started learning it. It seemed like this massive unknown quantity, and I didn't even know where to get started. Then, quite by accident, I became the Executive Vice President of Sales for a mortgage bank. That fancy title boiled down to sales manager. It was my job to teach other people how to sell, but to do that first I needed to learn what marketing was.

Marketing is, in essence, figuring out who wants to buy what you're selling, then making sure they're aware it exists. I very quickly realized that marketing boiled down to three basic goals that fed into each other:

1. Drive Qualified Traffic to your product or service
2. Convert that traffic

3. Store as much of that traffic as possible
   for future sales

Qualified Traffic

So why is Qualified Traffic capitalized? Because just driving traffic won't help you. If you send tens of thousands of people to your book's sales page, but none of those people read, then none of them are going to buy it. You need to *qualify* the traffic you send. The more qualified your audience, the higher your conversion is.

Back in the dark ages (we called them the 90s) cable networks made a killing with advertising. Everyone from Taco Bell to Chase had commercials, and those commercials were broadcast across a variety of channels. Their conversion rate was terrible, because the vast majority of us had no interest in random pharmaceutical drugs, or a new lawnmower. But companies used them anyway, because even terrible conversion meant more sales.

Today we have a lot of tools that people in the 90s didn't have. The internet allows you to zero in on a specific audience with laser focus. You can figure out exactly who your target customer is, and make sure that only people like her will see your ad.

A great example of this is BookBub. If you run a BookBub ad they'll show your book to a whole bunch of self-*qualified* readers. Every one of those readers said they liked books like yours. That's why BookBub is so powerful. It is the epitome of driving Qualified Traffic.

Conversion

Converting traffic to either sales or mailing list signups is an art form. Everything and anything you do to achieve this falls under conversion. This includes your eye catching cover, your super snazzy title, your blurb, the first few chapters of your book, or in the case of mailing lists your entire squeeze page (which we'll talk more about in the mailing list chapter).

Conversion is typically measured as a ratio. For simplicity's sake, if you drive 10 people to your page and one of them buys your book you have a 10% conversion rate. One of your primary goals is getting that number up. Optimizing your entire process to raise that from 10 to 30% will *triple* your sales.

This is why the packaging chapter is so important.

Capturing Traffic

Most newer authors are more excited about sales numbers than mailing list signups. I know I was. I didn't take mailing lists nearly as seriously as I should have, and that really hurt me in the beginning. I followed the prevailing wisdom of the day, which was writing a reader magnet and linking it in both the front and back matter of my books (and you should absolutely do the same). But that's *all* I did.

Today I understand that every mailing list sign up is far more valuable than a single sale. Each one represents a piece of Qualified Traffic, the building block of marketing. More importantly, these blocks are *highly* qualified. These are people who like *my* books, and are therefore very likely to buy more of them.

If you accumulate enough of these blocks a single email can sell thousands of copies. It can convince fans to leave dozens of reviews. Your mailing list is the foundation of your career, because it completes the marketing cycle. With a massive list you can make every product a success, and your success scales as your list grows.

When I had a hundred people I saw a little blip in sales. When I hit a thousand I could guarantee a book would break the top #3,000 on Amazon. What will that look like when I have ten thousand people on my list? Or fifty?

Applying This to Your Launch

I started *Launch to Market* with these three principles, because it's important that you understand that your launch's success isn't measured in sales. It's measured in platform. The more mailing list signups you get, the stronger every launch will be.

If you sold 10,000 copies in the first week, but didn't capture people's emails, how will any of them know about the sequel when it comes out? Or the books you're writing in 2025?

Before we launch your book we need to make sure you have all three principles covered. Drive that traffic, convert it, and make sure you're capturing it.

Exercise #2- Set up a mailing list if you do not already have one. Mailchimp is the simplest to use, but providers like Active Campaign are more powerful. Your list will be used in later chapters, so make sure you do this one!.

Bonus: Log into your website's admin portal and find their metrics. How many views and visitors do you average a day? How many of them click a link on your site that leads to your Amazon sales page? Can you think of anything that might raise either the traffic or conversion? How about both?

4

YOUR LAUNCH PLAN

Okay, the basics are covered. It's finally time to zero in on *your* launch. Launching a book requires a lot of preparation. Ideally you're reading this at least a month before you plan to launch yours. You want to have a highly detailed game plan long before you press that publish button.

There are three general phases you want to account for. **Launch Preparation, The Launch,** and **Autopilot.** I'll cover the specific pieces of each, and why they're important to the long term success of your book.

Launch Preparation

One of the things that will greatly aid your launch is building buzz among your potential audience. We do that by making them aware that the book exists *before* its available. This will make them more likely to purchase once it goes live.

Most people don't purchase something the first time they see it. Some need to see it as many as seven times before finally pressing that buy button. The sooner you get it on your readers' radar, the more sales you'll get at launch.

The Launch

Once all your preparation is complete, there are only a few steps to running the actual launch. This part is comparatively easy. Most of the heavy lifting is going to happen in the preparation stage, and the remaining work is all about getting the book set on autopilot.

Autopilot

One of the common misconceptions that carries over from traditional publishing is the idea that a book's launch makes or breaks its success. I've seen tons of books that flopped at launch, only to take off six months into release when the author did a rebranding.

Try to think of your book as a long term investment. It will still be selling in five years, and possibly in fifty. To that end, your goal is to set up a program that implements the three marketing principles. You want to keep getting your book in front of people, get them to buy it, and then collect their contact information so you give them the opportunity to buy your next book.

The goal is to put this all on autopilot, so your book is selling and adding mailing list subscribers without you doing anything. This frees you up to write the next book.

Exercise #3- Start a master document to plan your launch. I find that Excel works wonderfully for this, but use whatever tool is comfortable. Create an area for Launch Preparation, The Launch, and Autopilot. As you progress through the book, add to each of these sections. This will form the core of your final launch plan.

5

LAUNCH PREPARATION

Prior to launching your book you need to answer some pretty big questions. Where are you planning on selling it? Just Amazon (which is the easiest route), or every online retailer? How much will you charge for it? Should you do a preorder? How about advertising for the initial launch?

The answers will be different for every person asking the questions, but it's important to have *your* answers, and to know why those are the right answers for *you*. In this chapter we'll talk about the choices I made for *Destroyer,* and why I made them.

Amazon Exclusivity

You have two real choices as an independent author. You can either be exclusive to Amazon, or you can list your book everywhere. Other big retailers include Apple, Nook, Kobo, & GooglePlay. If you do go wide you can simplify the process by using a service like Draft2Digital to distribute your book everywhere at once.

Which should you do, and why?

If you are a new author, I recommend going exclusive with Amazon, at least for the first 90 days. The reason? Organic discoverability is much, much higher if you are enrolled in Amazon's Kindle Unlimited program. Readers can pick up your book for free, and you get paid based on the number of pages read. Every time someone borrows your book it counts as a sale, which pushes you higher in rank.

Higher rank means more eyeballs, which keeps your book selling. My first book debuted in Kindle Unlimited and I kept it there for six months. After I pulled it the rank dropped from #18,000 to #60,000 within 48 hours. That meant that the only people on Amazon finding my book were the ones that I was directing there through ads or word of month. Marketing was all on me.

The upside of being wide is that the *Deathless* Series sells everywhere, especially on Apple. I have readers around the world, which is wonderful for building a long term platform. It means less shorter term profits, though, which is why so many authors steer clear of it.

I chose to enroll *Destroyer* in KU, but I will reassess that every three months. Eventually it will go wide, but only once the KU revenue drops significantly and I have more books in the series out.

Pricing

I listed Destroyer for 99 cents for the first five days of the launch. The book's product description told the reader that the sale would end on April 4th, which let them know they had a narrow window to get it for that price. This created scarcity, encouraging more people to click that buy button. However, this meant that I was only getting 35 cents a sale, instead of the $2.09 I'd get for a full price sale.

I sacrificed short term profit for long term visibility. With the book both available in KU and set to 99 cents it all but removed price as a barrier. Anyone who wanted the book could purchase it, and thousands did.

The book reached its peak on April 1st, and

once that rank began to fall I set it back to full price. I did this a few days before I'd originally planned to, because I knew I'd lose a ton of the initial revenue otherwise. It proved to be a smart decision. The book slid down to #700 by the end of the first week, but it also sold 120+ copies a day at full price.

Contrast this launch to the book you're holding. Launch to Market came out at full price, and *isn't* enrolled in Kindle Unlimited. It's still profitable, but it will never surge up the ranks in the same way Destroyer did.

So why didn't I put it in KU? Because KU pays on pages read, and this is a short book. I get $2.09 a sale, about 20 cents from a borrow. My fiction is much longer, so KU makes more sense. Consider the length of your book when you're deciding about Kindle Unlimited.

Pros and Cons of Preorders

There are both pros and cons to listing a preorder on Amazon. The pro is that readers can impulse buy your book instead of having to wait until it goes live. This is especially true of later books in a series, where people will finish book one and want to immediately purchase book two.

Preorders also keep your book on Amazon's hot new releases list longer. Normally your book is there for 30 days after launch, but if you have a 30 day preorder your book will appear there for 60 days. If you have a sizable following this can keep your book selling well even before it launches.

Lastly, preorders will mean that your book's 'also bought' section will populate before you launch. Your book will begin percolating throughout the Amazon ecosystem, which will help organic sales after it launches.

The con, on Amazon at least, is that preorders dilute launch momentum. Amazon counts a preorder on the day of the sale, so if people preorder your book they're not buying it at launch. This has come back to bite me twice, and led to *No Mere Zombie* launching with a whimper when it should have had a bang.

For *Destroyer* I compromised. I did a 7 day preorder. That was long enough to populate my also bought, built a little buzz around the book, but was short enough not to dilute my launch numbers. I didn't publicize the preorder in any way, which meant a trickle of organic sales every day.

Which route you choose is up to you. Preorders can be amazing, especially on other platforms than Amazon. Apple, for example, gives you credit for the sale both on the day the reader makes it, and again on the date when the book launches.

Should You Advertise the Launch?

This is another tough question. In my case I chose not to advertise the launch with book sites like Ereader News Today, AwesomeGang, or The Fussy Librarian. Doing so this early would have started the process of market saturation. In other words, you can only sell so many books using those advertisers, and every time you use them it will be a little weaker than the time before.

I wanted to save that advertising for my first Kindle Countdown Deal, something Amazon allows you to run once every 90 days if you are exclusive. That countdown deal will kick off the launch of the second book in my trilogy, and I want it to be as powerful as possible.

Your answer could be different. If you don't yet have an author platform advertising may be your only choice for building launch momentum, and if that's the case I suggest building it along the slow curve discussed in the following chapter. That's what I had to do with *No Such Thing As Werewolves*, my first novel. I used advertising early and often to strengthen the launch, because I had no platform.

Exposure Is Vital. Initial Exposure Isn't.

Getting your book in front of a sufficient number of people is the only real way to test it. You need to have hundreds or ideally thousands of pairs of eyes on your work. Only then can you see what a large segment of people think, and then learn from their opinions. The bad news is, you need a lot of sales to make this happen.

Here's the good news. Exposure is vital. *Immediate* exposure is not. You don't need to sell eight billion copies the first month. You can wait three or six months without losing much. That means it's never too late to run a big promo and get your book in front of a large group of people.

This is also why I recommended finding your tier back in chapter 2. If you're launching your first book, then no matter the outcome you're finding your tier. You can then start targeting the next tier, and eventually the next. That will take time, and that's okay. We're in this for the long haul.

Exercise #4- This one is easy! Get out your launch plan and record the following: Launch Date. Preorder (Y/N). Launch Price. Full Price.

Bonus: Schedule your first promotion on the launch plan. This can be at launch, especially if you have no other platform to use. If your 2nd book is coming out within 90 days consider that when scheduling.

6

THE SLOW CURVE

You'll hear me talk a lot about Amazon's algorithms, and it may not be clear to non-software people what those are or why they matter. The algorithms are, in essence, an artificial intelligence that figures out who to show your book to. If this AI decides a certain type of person will buy your book, then it will show it to as many of those people as possible.

They'll send out mailers telling people that they might like your book. When people come to Amazon's home page, your book will be displayed to the type of people ZonBot thinks will buy it. As long as people keep buying it ZonBot is happy to keep telling more.

Until you reach the cliffs of despair.

The Cliffs of Despair

Amazon has three cliffs that your book will go over. The 30, 60, and 90 day cliffs. At the end of 30 days your book is no longer on the Hot New Releases list, which reduces its visibility. This is the only verifiable cliff, because you can see yourself go over it. The next two are anecdotal, but I've heard them from every author I know, and I've experienced them myself.

At the end of 60 days Amazon will reduce the frequency at which it notifies people via email that they might like your book. That happens again at the end of 90 days. After that your book is more or less on its own. You can still get Amazon to notice it, but it takes a LOT more work to do so. The burden of sales then falls on you, which is why it's so important to maximize the first three months after launch. The best way to do that is to release your sequels no more than three months apart.

But how do you maximize your first three months?

The Slow Curve

Amazon's algorithm is ever changing, and anyone telling you that they know exactly how it works is either lying or an Amazon engineer. The algo is a black box, but that's okay. We don't need to know exactly how it functions so long as we can observe its behavior. I've been observing this behavior for a year and a half, from the perspective of a data scientist.

What I've seen over and over is that Amazon respects the slow curve over the sudden spike. In other words, if you sell 2,000 books today, but only 50 tomorrow, then Amazon will assume that 2,000 sales was an anomaly, and will give it far less weight. Your rank is constantly decaying, and the older the sale the less it matters. After a few days Amazon barely remembers your 2,000 sale spike.

If, on the other hand, you have a slow curve... Amazon will sit up and take notice. A slow curve is simply an increasing number of daily sales. Like so:

Day 1- 5 sales
Day 2- 7 Sales
Day 3- 10 Sales
Day 4- 12 Sales
Day 5- 18 Sales
Days 6- 80 Sales

If Amazon sees this kind of curve, ZonBot assumes people are liking your book. The longer this upward trending curve, the more momentum Amazon will put behind your book. It will try to keep that push going until it figures out two things:

1. Your book's real target audience
2. Your book's settling point

Amazon tracks a variety of metrics about its audience, and is probably one of the best companies in the world at doing this. It knows the age, sex, purchasing history, and location of anyone who buys one of your books. The algorithm will start searching for people who match that target audience, and Amazon will periodically send out mailers showing your book (and usually a few others) to people it thinks will buy them.

Your book may find a sales equilibrium of around 10 copies a day, which at the time of this writing would give it a rank of about #25,000 in the store. If Amazon realizes this, then it will try to keep your book around that equilibrium. If you suddenly sell more copies, it will resist your rank improving. If you sell a few less, it won't penalize you as much. Basically, Amazon is taking the average and trying to keep your book near it.

Your goal with a slow curve is to get Amazon to think your settling point is as high as possible. For *Destroyer* that settling point was around #700 in the store, which means about 100 sales a day and about 35,000 pages read. That's definitely my best launch ever. For contrast *No Such Thing As Werewolves* was about 12 sales a day, and about 2,900 pages. Its settling rank was around #6,000.

Destroyer took me from tier IV to tier III.

Building Your Curve

To build a slow curve you want to put your strongest promotion at the end. Whatever your strongest promotion is (your huge list, BookBub, etc) is your promo anchor. That anchor should be the last day of your promo.

You lead up to your promo anchor with smaller sites. If you're doing book advertising sites that might mean putting The Fussy Librarian on day 1, AwesomeGang on day 2, and Ereader News Today on day 3. It could also mean utilizing mailing list segmentation, which we'll cover in the chapter on mailing lists.

Exercise #5- Get out your launch plan, and create a section called promotion. Write down every last way you can think of to promote your book. This should include communities you're a part of, social media, advertising sites, mailing lists, and anything else you're fairly sure might result in a sale. Rank these according to potential impact, and start building a curve from weakest on day 1 to strongest on day 5.

7

PACKAGING

I deally you're reading this a month or two before you launch your book. In a perfect world you've already read *Write to Market*. *Write to Market* explains how to write and package your book in a way that will resonate with readers.

If you haven't read it (and don't want to) here's the part that's most relevant to you. Your **cover, blurb,** and **look inside** are the yard stick by which your book is measured by online consumers. I'm only going to give a quick overview here. If you want more, check out *Write to Market*.

Don't Judge a Book By Its Cover

Bullshit. This is the worst lie writers were taught

growing up. Your cover is the first and most important line of defense in the war of art.

When people go to Amazon (or any other online retailer) they see your book as a tiny thumbnail among a sea of other books. If your cover doesn't draw their eye, you've already lost the war. Some other cover DID attract their eye, and they clicked that book instead. Even if you have a beautiful cover, it has to translate well as a thumbnail.

Check out *Destroyer* on Amazon. Notice that you can make out the well lit ship in the thumbnail. Notice the green dominating the cover. These draw the eye. Lest you think I get everything right (far from it), let me share a cautionary tale.

The cover you see on Destroyer was NOT the original one. I paid the renowned Tom Edwards a little over $750 to make the first cover I commissioned. The art is breathtaking at full size, but the ugly truth was that it was simply too dark as a thumbnail. It didn't draw the eye.

So I shelled out another $1,000 to get the cover you see on the book now. Was it worth it? Hell yes. Double hell yes. I learned that lesson the hard way with *Hero Born*. The cover for that book is just okay. It isn't amazing, and it doesn't draw the eye. That's a huge reason why *Hero Born* flopped, and I strongly suspect that if I replaced the cover I'd see an immediate spike in sales.

Your cover is the single best investment of resources you can make. If you're not good at judging what makes a great cover, find people who are before getting yours made.

Titles

After the cover, your title is the next line of defense. It had better raise a question or draw a connection in the reader's mind, or again they're clicking on another book that does. Your title needs to fit the genre. It needs to conform to reader expectations, so hearing it makes them curious.

Great examples? *The Atlantis Gene.* That title got me to click on the book, because it conveyed technothriller with a side of Dan Brown. For my own books, *Write to Market*, *5,000 Words Per Hour*, and *No Such Thing As Werewolves* all tell you exactly what to expect.

Make sure your title does its job.

Blurb

If your title and cover convinced your potential customer to click on your product page, the blurb becomes the next line of defense. This is your chance to convey the essence of your story to the reader. If it doesn't excite them, they've already clicked the back button.

The best way to craft your blurb is to find other successful books in your genre. What does their blurb look like? What elements does it reference? Craft something similar for yours, but make it unique to your story. Then, get people who like that genre to read your blurb. Would they read that book? If not, go back to the drawing board, or find a service like Best Page Forward to help you craft a better one.

Look Inside

Amazon's Look Inside feature shows your first several chapters to the reader, right there on the site. They can read the entire first act or so of your book, and many of them will do exactly that.

Your first few chapters need to be engaging, free of typos, and formatted well...if any of those pieces is missing you just lost a sale. If, on the other hand, your first few chapters are gripping, then your book is primed to take off like a rocket.

Exercise #6- Review your book's cover, and be honest. Is this on par with the best books in your genre, or is it just okay? How about your title? Why did you pick it? Does it mean anything to someone who hasn't read your book? How about your first few chapters? Are they absolutely amazing?

Bonus: Get someone (or an entire community of someones) to review your cover, title, and first chapter. Do they think it's amazing? If not, what can you tweak before launch?

8

KEYWORDS AND CATEGORIES

K eywords and Categories are often brought up, so I decided to add a short chapter explaining what they are and why they are important. The good news is that Amazon is incredibly helpful to authors, so if you're a little lost don't hesitate to reach out to them for assistance.

This chapter only provides the basics. Entire books have been written on keywords, and they're a powerful tool in your marketing arsenal.

Keywords

Amazon allows you to use seven keywords associated with your book. Users who search for that particular keyword are more likely to find your book. However, keywords can also be used to add your book to various subcategories. Ideally, you want to mix your seven between categories and searchable terms. Categories are explained below.

If you're unsure what to use for a searchable term, just consider what someone looking for a book like yours might type into the search bar. In my case, I started with 'Werewolf Horror'. As soon as I typed that in Amazon presented Werewolf Horror Novel as a suggestion. That became my first keyword, because if Amazon suggests it to me they'll suggest it to other people too.

Those autocomplete terms are a godsend, if you use them correctly. It can take some trial and error, but it's worth making sure you have at least a few of these terms. Well placed ones can ensure that your book comes up on the first page of search results, and that can mean real sales very quickly.

Categories and Subcategories

Amazon allows you to pick two main categories when setting up your book. Examples include Literature & Fiction —> Horror, Science Fiction & Fantasy —> Super Hero.

Categories are the browsable areas of Amazon. People can look at all Suspense novels, then drill down into Vampire Suspense subcategory. If you wanted to be one of the books readers saw there, then you'd have two choices. You could use one of your categories, or you could add Vampire as a keyword. This is how people end up with 5-6 categories on their product page.

People often ask how many of their keywords should go to categories. The answer is as many as it takes to get in the *right* categories. My novel *Destroyer* is in five categories, where *No Such Thing As Werewolves* is in three. What you do depends largely on the genre you're writing for, but whatever that is you should be familiar with all the relevant categories.

Exercise #7- This one is a two parter with no bonus. Take both these actions. Go to Amazon and experiment with searchable keywords until you find a list of search terms you can use that would lead readers to books like yours. Write down the list.

Browse the Amazon subcategories you want to be in until you're certain you've identified all of them. Go to KDP's help page (found in your KDP dashboard on the upper right) to see the list of what keywords you need to use in order to be in those categories.

9

READER MAGNET

Welcome to the shortest chapter in the book. I made it a chapter, because Reader Magnets are important enough to warrant it. They're powerful, powerful, tools every author should use.

Reader magnet is a term coined by Nick Stephenson, who released a free ebook of the same name. I highly recommend reading it before you try to implement a reader magnet, but this chapter will give you the basics of what they are and how to use them.

The content marketing industry is far more mature than self-publishing. They have a myriad of resources available, things we just haven't learned about selling books yet. Smart authors are turning to content marketing to learn their techniques.

Reader magnets are an adaptation of Lead Magnets. A lead magnet is, simply put, a bribe to get someone to give you their email address. It can be your series artwork, character sheets, a free PDF, a short story, or anything else that will convince people to join your list.

The best lead magnets have a high conversion rate, and they also drive highly Qualified Traffic.

Exiled

Let's use my reader magnet for *Destroyer* as an example. *Exiled* is a 12,000 word short story. Readers can sign up on my website, or click the front / back matter of the book to get *Exiled*. My conversion rate has been amazing, and in the first month I accumulated over a thousand mailing list signups.

Why? Because I chose *the right* reader magnet. *Exiled* was meticulously crafted. In the novel *Destroyer* I raise questions in the narrative. How did Nolan end up where he is, exiled to the dregs of the fleet? What happened between him and Kathryn that put him there? This short story answers those questions. If people read *Destroyer* and liked it, then they'll want to answer that question.

That's *exactly* the person I want on my list. If they liked the book enough to want the prequel, then they'll almost certainly buy the sequel. *Exiled* attracts the right reader, and rewards them with a fun story. They get what they want, and I get to market them more books that they'll love. Win / win.

Exercise #8- Brainstorm a reader magnet. Is there a narrative question you could answer with a short story? Something readers will love? If not, can you give them a character sheet, fan artwork, or something else relevant to them?

Bonus: Actually create that reader magnet.

10

THE LAUNCH

If you've done the work to this point, then you now have a basic launch plan. Assuming you're reading this all in one sitting, then here's what you're expected to have at least brainstormed by now:

1. Amazing packaging
2. Targeted keywords
3. Your reader magnet
4. Promotion staggered to create a slow curve

Is any part of that not done? If so, I'd recommend holding off on your launch. Unless you are locked into a pre-order date it's worth waiting until you're ready. You only get one chance to launch your book the right way. Kick this part's ass, and your book could jump you a tier. Failure isn't the end of the world, but it is a wasted opportunity.

ARCs and Review Copies

One of the things that will add legitimacy to your book is reviews. Getting the first few can be tricky, so I lean on my mailing list(s) to help.

I send advanced review copies to readers about two weeks before a book comes out. I do this both to give them time to read, and because they generally find any typos. I skipped this part of the process when I released *Destroyer*, and ended up with some egg on my face as you read in the case study chapter.

Double Check Your Launch Schedule

Double check your launch to make sure it is all properly scheduled. When are you emailing your list? Are you segmenting it (explained in chapter 14)? Do you have a promo anchor, and if so is it at the end of your slow curve? What social media are you using when? It should all be recorded, and anyone who needs to be notified should be in the loop.

If you're like me you'll be tempted to tell everyone the second the book is live. Resist this impulse. If all your promo drops at once it will lose effectiveness with the Amazon algorithms. You're looking to build a trend, not a spike.

Publication Paralysis

I have quite a few writer friends who have been sitting on their manuscript for months. They could publish it, but they'd rather give it one more pass. They'd like to tweak their keywords a little more, or polish the first chapter. That path is dangerous.

I applaud preparedness, but it can lead to paralysis. Don't let that be you. When you are *reasonably* sure you are ready, don't be afraid. Hit that publish button. No matter what happens you'll learn from it, and if you don't press publish you'll never sell a single book.

Be ready, then press that publish button.

Spreading the Buzz

Your chief responsibility during a launch is to spread the buzz you began during the preparation phase. This can be accomplished via social media, blog posts, podcasts, or anywhere else you have a connection with your audience. Cover reveals are a great way to do this, especially if you have an eye catching cover (you do, right?). All of that should be scheduled on your launch plan.

This buzz should be spread over a period of days, just like your promotion. You also want to be careful about frequency. I see many authors tweet every 4-6 hours about a launch. Personally, I avoid doing that. I'll mention it only once on Facebook or Twitter. After that I wait for fans to tweet or post, then respond and share those posts.

I do this, both because it feels more genuine, and because I don't think repeatedly spamming 'buy my book' is effective. I hate seeing it, and suspect most of my audience does too. So I don't do it.

Fixing Problems

The bigger your launch, the more likely you encounter a problem. The faster you publish, the more likely these problems are. I'm an advocate of rapid publishing, but I'm also aware that it comes with a cost.

Earlier, I mentioned a serious error in the final draft that went out to thousands of readers. In the last chapter I substituted the wrong character name. Every instance where it should have been one character it was another. Yikes, talk about embarrassing.

It happened, because I added the chapter after getting it back from my editor. Tammi was horrified, of course. I wrote a new epilogue, and uploaded the book to Amazon. No one but me ever saw that chapter, which is how I ended up with the error.

Over fifty people brought the problem to my attention, and several pointed it out in reviews. I corrected the error, and uploaded a new version within minutes. A few hours later it was approved, and everyone who ever buys the book going forward will get the corrected version. We can fix our work in the same way I used to fix software.

Almost every launch has an issue. All we have to do is fix it, and move on. It can be tempting to obsess on it, but once you've done what you can to solve the problem try to let it go. We won't even remember it in a few months.

~

Exercise #9- Finalize your book launch plan. What emails are you sending out and when? Are you posting on any forums? Write down every thing you're doing during launch week, and schedule it meticulously. This will make it simple to run your launch.

11

AUTOPILOT

A t long last we reach the secret sauce, the thing that will make or break your long term career as an author. Putting your marketing on autopilot.

The next four chapters reveal the big truth of being an author in today's digital world. Twenty years ago an author's book had a literal shelf life. There was a limited amount of space on shelves in book stores, and after your book stopped selling it was removed. It fell into obscurity, and eventually out of print.

Today your books are in print forever. They never disappear, and you can always reach new fans with them. That's a *huge* change for authors, because it means you should still be seeking readers for your first book after you've released your fortieth. The rest of the book details how you can put that process on autopilot. Your book will continue to sell, to generate mailing list signups, and to lead people to your other books.

If you master this piece, you'll ensure you always make a good living. What if every book you ever put out averaged five hundred dollars a month for the rest of your life? Putting your books on autopilot can make that happen. Below I'll give you a few examples of people doing exactly that.

The Tale of Mark Cooper

Mark Cooper last published a novel in December of 2013. That means it's been two and a half years since he released a new book, yet he is still making a comfortable living as an author.

Mark does this because he's put his books on autopilot. Using Facebook ads, multiple platforms, and the occasional promotion Mark has kept his books selling. He keeps collecting email addresses, and introducing new readers to his books.

He's the most exemplary example I can think of

that has done everything right for promotion. Mark is exactly who we want to emulate.

The Tale of Robert Jordan

I considered listing another indie as a case study, but I wanted to drive home the long term power putting your book on autopilot can have. I wanted to show you what could happen after decades.

Robert Jordan wrote *The Eye of the World* in November of 1990. *A Memory of Light*, the 14th and final book in *The Wheel of Time* series, was released on December of 2013, twenty three years later. As expected, *A Memory of Light* sold millions of copies, but that's not the important take away here.

The Eye of the World is still ranked #4,000 in the Amazon store. After 23 years, the beginning of this series is still pulling in a LOT of new readers. Book two is ranked at #5,200 in the store, and other volumes have a similar rank. New people find the series, and then a lot of them read the whole thing.

That's one hell of a sales funnel. Imagine if they were capturing reader's emails with a Wheel of Time Reader Magnet.

Our whole goal is to set up a similar system. We want to set up streams of readers who are continuously discovering our books. There are many different tactics to doing that, and some vary from genre to genre.

Over the next few chapters we'll discuss Product Funnels, Tracking, the all powerful Mailing List, and some out of the box thinking for finding new readers. Combining all of them can take your career to the next level.

Exercise #10- Go to Amazon and look at the category or categories matching your book. Search the top 20 and look at the release date for each. Can you find any books that are selling a ton of copies more than a year after release? Write down those books. These will become the case studies you use to position your own book for long term success.

Figure out what they're doing, and do as much of the same as is reasonably possible.

Bonus: Subscribe to the authors of these books via

their author pages on Amazon. Each time you receive a release email from them, go back to the OLD book and see how well it's doing.

12

PRODUCT FUNNELS

A product funnel is wide at one end, and narrows down to a single point on the other (like a funnel =p). The narrowest point is where someone buys your book, or signs up to your mailing list. How you get them from discovering you to your desired sale / signup *is* your product funnel.

How well you master the creation of these funnels will determine your long term success as an author. You must attract a large amount of traffic into your funnel, convert them into readers, then gather their email addresses.

This isn't a unique idea, nor is it one I invented. Mark Dawson and Nick Stephenson have both proved this in the author world, and it existed in content marketing for two decades. It was part of other industries long before that.

My whole long term strategy lies around the optimization of the lead process. How can I get more readers into my funnel, and how can I optimize my funnel so more of them convert?

For our purposes there are three parts to master

1. Awareness
2. Squeeze page
3. Delivery

Our goal is to build awareness by driving qualified traffic to the squeeze page. Once a reader converts (signs up), we need a seamless delivery so our relationship is established in a positive way.

Awareness

This goes right back to Qualified Traffic. Specifically, we're after the low hanging fruit. Do you have a Goodreads Profile? How about Twitter or Instagram? You're on Facebook, right? Because your readers are in all those places.

You don't need to spend a ton of time there, but

having a profile gives your fans something to latch onto. I barely use Twitter, but I make sure to reply to fans who reach out. It happens several times a week, and from those infrequent interactions I've gradually built up to 400 followers. That's 400 people I would never have reached if I didn't have an account.

Make sure you've considered every type of social media, and have created accounts for every one that makes sense. Also make sure those social media all tie back to a central location, like your website. Setting that up can take a little time, but once it's done you're on autopilot.

All sorts of neat little things start happening. My blog posts are pushed directly to Goodreads. My YouTube videos are announced on Twitter. Every one of these little things is a tiny stream leading readers into my funnel.

Lead Pages

The industry refers to Lead Pages as squeeze pages. I hate the term squeeze page. It make it sound like we're fleecing someone, and it's part of the reason I shy away from a lot of the content marketing resources I've run across. They're more concerned with separating people from their money than they are making them aware of a great product.

So what is a Lead Page, exactly? Assuming you have a mailing list, you had to design a landing page where people could sign up. That page is your Lead Page. You want to optimize the crap out of it, until you've maximized conversion. In other words, we want every possible sign up.

You do that by simplifying the page into these parts:

1. What do **they get** for signing up?
2. What's their **email address**?

That's it. Mine has the cover of *Exiled*, two sentences about the reader magnet, and a box for their email address. I don't ask for their name, because people hate giving out personal information. The more complex you make your Lead Page, the less likely someone is to sign up. Get the basics right, and you'll increase conversion dramatically.

The Real Lead Pages

In listening to Pat Flynn's Smart Passive Income

podcast I stumbled across a company called Lead Pages. Lead Pages creates custom landing pages for you. If that doesn't sound exciting, consider this. You've set up your Mailchimp, Aweber, or Active Campaign account. You've got a mailing list, and you built your basic lead page as described above.

You get 10 signups a day. Pretty cool, right? What if an optimized Lead Page brought that up to fifteen? Imagine the difference amplified over a year. That's another eighteen hundred email addresses over the course of a year.

Small tweaks matter.

Delivery

This is the part I learned the most about during the launch of *Destroyer*. I used Mailchimp to distribute an ePub version of my reader magnet. Many people were unable to open that format, and I get requests every day to help them side load the book onto their kindle. This is painful for them and time consuming for me. It doesn't help anyone, and it leads to unhappy readers.

So I'm moving to BookFunnel. BookFunnel will deliver the correct format of your book to each user, and help them load it onto their device. If a user can't load it, they get BookFunnel's tech support instead of your email. Win / win. They get competent help, and you get to keep writing.

I'd heard a lot about the company, but had never prioritized setting it up. *Destroyer*'s launch galvanized me, and I finally put my BookFunnel into place. I can't say from personal experience that it's as awesome as it sounds, but a lot of my friends swear by it.

Exercise #II- Build your lead page, either using the tools offered by your mailing list provider, or by setting up a lead page account.

Bonus: Before setting up your lead page check out the signups for five of your favorite authors. What elements do they use? Can you use similar elements?

13

TRACKING

I n *5,000 Words Per Hour* I had a chapter on tracking. In that chapter I used a quote. What can be tracked, can be improved. That's more true than ever with marketing. *Everything* must be tracked, or marketing will make you feel like you're fumbling about in the dark...on lava.

There are a lot of important metrics in marketing, ranging from how much website traffic you're getting, to how many people are clicking your affiliate links, to how low your cost per click is on ads.

This chapter will break down each type of metric, and suggest tools for tracking and improving them.

Facebook / Amazon / Goodreads / Google Ads

We'll start with the one you're most likely familiar with, ads. There are many different flavors of ads, but the most talked about ones are Facebook ads, by far. All four types have a few things in common.

You bid for clicks, meaning you only pay if someone clicks your ad. The cost of that click is referred to as a CPC (cost per click). Your goal with these ads is to raise your conversion, and to lower your CPC. The cheaper the CPC the more people see your ad for the same cost. Optimizing this will help you get that coveted auto-pilot turned on.

But how do you do that? Lots and lots of *expensive* experimentation. You try a variety of ads with different images and copy, and you see which ones have a low CPC. Those survive. The rest you kill off. This is repeated endlessly, and if you don't enjoy the process it will make you stab yourself in the eye with a pen.

Here's the great news. You don't need to run ads to be successful. If learning these platforms isn't on your radar, that's okay. They will not make or break your book, merely augment your success. If you can work them in eventually, wonderful. Just don't feel obligated to, especially if there are other things you can work on.

Website Metrics

I use Wordpress, so everything I'm about to say is specific to that platform. That said, the other site generation / hosting sites all have their own flavor of metrics. You should be able to find this data on yours.

- Unique Visitors per day
- Views per day
- External clicks

Wordpress presents a nifty little graph that shows your days, weeks, months, or years for each of these metrics. You can see how many people came, which pages they read, and how many people clicked on things like your affiliate links for your books.

Your goal should be to increase all three. Doing that is simple, but not easy. Figure out what kind of content your audience is interested in, and then give it to them. This part cannot be phoned in, either.

A great example is free fiction. Can you write some short stories relating to your series? Great! Put them up for free. See how your audience reacts. Do they visit those pages? Does your traffic spike when you post one? Awesome! Keep posting more of that.

I recently started a YouTube channel to host the 21 Day Novel Challenge Videos. I started adding series on craft, motivation, and marketing. I very quickly realized that the days I posted Motivation videos I had the highest spike in traffic. The next highest was craft. Marketing was a distant third.

Guess what type of content I'll be focusing on going forward?

Sales Data

You're probably already tracking your sales, but if you aren't I'd encourage you to start. Book Report is a fabulous tool, which connects directly to your Amazon account. It shows you a much more granular breakdown of sales, so you can see when you have spikes, and how long tails are. You can also see what percentage of income each book accounts for.

This is important, because over time you'll learn from this data. You'll see how sales fall over a period of months, then years. You'll see how promotions push that back up, and how long they push it back up for. That data will teach you, but before you can analyze it you have to track it.

Whether you use your own spreadsheet, Quick-books, Book Report, or some other tool, just make sure you're tracking!

Exercise #12- Log into your website and check your metrics. How many people have clicked an Amazon link this month? How could you optimize your site to increase that? Is another author in your genre doing a great job there? What can you mine from their page to improve yours?

14

MAILING LISTS

B y now, I'm sure you understand why mailing lists are important, but I'm going to restate it anyway. Mailing lists are vital. Absolutely vital. This is the single most valuable asset you have right now, even more so than your backlist.

Why?

The Importance of Mailing Lists

Amazon could decide tomorrow that you need an agent to upload a book. Or they could dramatically cut what we're getting paid. Or they could suddenly be eclipsed by another major player. Hey, it could happen. Microsoft was once considered invincible, and Apple was a laughing stock.

Even if it doesn't, we need to remember Amazon's motivation. They want happy readers, not writers. They're going to do whatever they can to protect their bottom line, and they understand the same marketing principles you're learning here. No one is better at retaining customer information, not even Facebook.

It's in Amazon's best interest to take that a step further by preventing you from capturing that same information. They want customers finding products through them, not you. This is why you see small changes, like them popping up a request to rate the book before your back matter link to your mailing list. They want to prevent readers from seeing it, but we need to make sure they do.

If you set up a great funnel, you're Amazon independent. You can send a single email and have thousands of sales across multiple platforms. But to do that you first need a list. Your list frees you. It guarantees that you can reach your audience, no matter what Amazon or any other retailer does.

Using Segmentation

You'll often hear people bring up segmentation, and it may not be immediately clear what they mean. Segmentation is quite simply using segments of your mailing list. When you segment, you can send specific emails to subsets of your list. This can include reaching out only to highly engaged people, or emailing disengaged people to warn them you're about to remove them.

From an advertising standpoint segmentation means you don't need to send an email to everyone at once. You can break up your list into segments, and then send an email to segments over time. For my last launch I did a segment every 12 hours, beginning with the least engaged. This helped build my slow curve.

Growing Your List

There are two main components to list growth, and both have already been touched on. First, you need a GREAT reader magnet. Or, a series of reader magnets. I have several, depending on which audience I'm trying to attract.

Second, you need a highly visible lead page. Check out Mark Dawson's site at markdawson.com.

He does an amazing job of askir
and he's the one I'm striving to er
the link (or create a separate on
front and back matter of your boo

    If you can't do something that
the bat, that's fine. Get a Lead Page set up. Even a
bad one is better than none, and I'm surprised by
how well my clunky Mailchimp landing page
converted.

Autoresponder Sequences

This is another term that many people are mysti-
fied by. An auto responder sends an email automatically. You set a series of conditions, and when
those conditions are met your email provider sends
pre-created emails automatically. This is an
extremely powerful tool, especially if you're using
one of the more robust providers like Active
Campaign.

    Here's the sequence I've set up for Destroyer:

- **Immediately**- Send welcome email to
link with free book

hours later- Send email making sure
they're able to open the book
- **1 Week**- Email them to ask if they enjoyed
the prequel. Mention that they can read
book two early if they join the ARC
program.

I have a slightly different sequence for people who
sign up via the website versus those in the back
matter. I have an entirely separate one for my *Deathless* series, and a third one for my *Write Faster, Write
Smarter* series.

Autoresponder sequences should be tailored to
the audience, and their results should be tracked. If
you see a bunch of unsubscribes after a certain
autoresponder goes out, then maybe you can puzzle
out why. What was the content?

Likewise, you can see which ones are open and
acted upon the most. Most of your emails will have a
CTA (call to action), which involves the reader
clicking on a link to an external resource. If more
people like your videos, then put out more videos. If
they love your short stories, can you give
them more?

Your audience will be unique to you, but if you learn it, then you can ensure you automatically deliver content they find valuable. This is a massive step along the path to auto-piloting your growth.

Using Your List

The most obvious use of your list is to announce your next book. It's also one of the most effective. You'll get massive engagement from your audience, because the whole reason most signed up was to hear about the next book. The larger your list, the more people just ran out and bought your new release. But that isn't the only use.

ARC Reader Segment

Every author hopes for a flurry of reviews after a book goes live. It makes your book more legitimate, and indirectly affects sales. Getting the first ten can be a real struggle, especially for your first book.

Your mailing list can take away the pain. My welcome email lets readers know about my ARC program. They get a free copy of the book two weeks before it goes live. In exchange, they leave an honest review. To prove they are honoring the program I ask them to send me a link or screenshot of the review if they want to stay in the program for the next book.

The larger my list has grown, the more reviews I get right after launch. That helps enormously, but there's another benefit. ARC readers often spot the last few pesky typos, which lets you correct them before releasing to the public.

Surveys

Data is powerful, and hearing what your fans are interested in can help you decide what path your career will take. Do they really want to read your epic fantasy? What other authors do they enjoy that they consider similar to you?

You can learn all sorts of things, and forge connections with your list in the process. People like being heard, and knowing that you're listening makes them more engaged. Not many authors do this, and it really stands out.

∾

Exercise #13- Create or update your first autoresponder sequence. Are you sending a welcome email? How about checking in with fans? Add at least one email to the sequence.

Bonus: Tell your readers about your ARC program, and see how many are willing to join. Use this team to launch your next book.

15

LONG TERM STRATEGIES

The final chapters of my books almost always have the same message. I end with it, because it is so important. The message is simply that this is a long journey. Whatever happens with your next book, it's just a brick in your fortress. You'll keep laying bricks, and keep getting better at it. You'll jump tiers, and you'll eventually make a great living at this (if you aren't already).

The key to doing that is setting up a sustainable career. You're going to hear all sorts of advice. People you trust are going to say you must do X or that Y is the only way to make it to the next level. In the end, the people who constantly experimented and never gave up are the ones who go the distance.

Your whole goal behind whatever launch you're doing next should be laying another brick in your fortress. Build it a little taller, and then make another brick. Don't get bogged down in what happens with that single brick, good or bad.

Social Media Use

People have told me to use everything from Twitter to Instagram to LinkedIn. They expound the virtues of each, and talk about how I could find so many readers if I spent some time there. Every last one of them is right, but here's the rub.

I'd have to spend time there. I don't, because I don't enjoy those platforms. If I spent time there trying to hawk my books the users of those platforms would sense it. It wouldn't be authentic, and readers can smell a fake.

So I only use platforms I enjoy. I highly recommend picking 2-3 you really enjoy. In my case those are Facebook, Reddit, Kboards, and a few smaller forums. I've recently delved into YouTube as well, which has been surprisingly fun.

That's the key. Fun. I like those platforms, so using them is natural. Which ones do you enjoy? Can you try another to see if you like it?

Compound Interest

Most of us are familiar with the idea of compound interest. It's how depositing $200,000 into retirement can become $2,000,000 over the course of a few decades.

We need to take the same approach to growing our brand. Every mailing list signup, every sale, it all adds up. Each launch is a little stronger than the last, because your list is larger. Your reader base is larger. You're more well known. Your writing is better.

It's a long slow process, but boy does the power increase over time. I had 50 people on my list my first month. By the time I launched book two I had almost 400 people. Book three launched to over a thousand people. That number keeps growing and growing, and I plan to pass 10,000 this year. Next year I'm aiming for a hundred thousand.

Succeed or fail, I'll keep growing my platform, and I'll keep selling more books as a result. Take the long view. Be patient, but also mindful. Look for ways you can optimize and improve, then give those tweaks time to show results.

Authenticity

This is the last section in the last chapter, because this is the note I want to leave you with. Be authentic. Do not compromise your morals, because those shortcuts aren't worth it.

We live in a jaded, cynical world. Especially where the internet is concerned. People are out to screw other people, and most everyone assumes you're trying to take advantage of them when you first meet. This makes marketing difficult, because people's guard is already up. Authenticity is how you earn their trust.

Prove to them that you're a good person, and that you're more interested in helping others than selling books. This cannot be forced. You cannot pretend to be authentic. People will know, they're more canny than many of us expect. They can spot the fakes, the people pretending to belong in a community because they have an agenda. Don't be that guy (or girl).

When you are seeking readers, you need to be interested in the same things they are. Find out where they hang out, and become a part of their tribe. If you write about the things they love, it shouldn't be hard for you to do, since you're probably into the same things (or why are you writing about it?).

This is a long slow road, but it leads to immense success. People remember authenticity. They remember people who help, and who give of themselves. Doors begin to open. People do you favors without asking. They want to see you succeed, because you've helped them succeed.

Be your highest, best self. And sell a lot of books.

Exercise #14- This may be the hardest exercise in the book, especially for newer authors. Find a mentee. This should be an author with less experience than you. Maybe it's a friend who writes, but isn't sure how to get to the next level. Offer them encouragement, and help them find the resources they need to get where you are.

WHAT NOW?

Congratulations, you've completed the entire book. Beyond this page are a full list of the exercises, but before we get there I want to take one final opportunity to talk about your launch.

The earlier in your career you are, the more this launch feels like it represents your entire career. My whole world was wrapped up in the success of my first book, and my mood rose and fell based on that success. Don't be like I was. Don't check your sales graphs endlessly. Set up your launch, execute it, and then move on to the next book.

It's okay to take a little time to celebrate, but dwelling on any one book is the surest way I know to lose momentum. Momentum is vital. Do what you can to keep yours.

If you haven't already done so please consider

taking a look at the other *Write Smarter, Write Faster* books. They include *5,000 Words Per Hour, Lifelong Writing Habit*, and *Write to Market*. Each fills a very specific role in helping you build a sustainable career, and if you liked *Launch to Market* you'll find them very similar.

Either way, thank you for taking this journey with me. If you have questions or comments, shoot me an email to chris@chrisfoxwrites.com. I can't answer every email any more, but I'll do my best to get to yours!

-Chris

EXERCISES

Exercise #1- Set a reminder on your phone for the marketing action you're going to take tomorrow. How will you improve? Maybe it's reading this book. Commit to that action. Make sure it gets done.

Bonus: Repeat this process every day for the next week. At the end of the week measure where you are, versus where you were when you started. What did you accomplish?

Bonus II: Write down your best Tier.

Exercise #2- Set up a mailing list if you do not already have one. Mailchimp is the simplest to use, but providers like Active Campaign are more powerful. Your list will be used in later chapters, so make sure you do this one!.

Bonus: Log into your website's admin portal and find their metrics. How many views and visitors do you average a day? How many of them click a link on your site that leads to your Amazon sales page? Can you think of anything that might raise either the traffic or conversion? How about both?

Exercise #3- Start a master document to plan your launch. I find that Excel works wonderfully for this, but use whatever tool is comfortable. Create an area for Launch Preparation, The Launch, and Autopilot. As you progress through the book, add to each of these sections. This will form the core of your final launch plan.

Exercise #4- This one is easy! Get out your launch plan and record the following: Launch Date. Preorder (Y/N). Launch Price. Full Price.

Bonus: Schedule your first promotion on the launch plan. This can be at launch, especially if you have no other platform to use. If your 2nd book is coming out within 90 days consider that when scheduling.

Exercise #5- Get out your launch plan, and create a section called promotion. Write down every last way you can think of to promote your book. This should include communities you're a part of, social media, advertising sites, mailing lists, and anything else you're fairly sure might result in a sale. Rank these according to potential impact, and start building a curve from weakest on day 1 to strongest on day 5.

Exercise #6- Review your book's cover, and be honest. Is this on par with the best books in your genre, or is it just okay? How about your title? Why did you pick it? Does it mean anything to someone who hasn't read your book? How about your first few chapters? Are they absolutely amazing?

Bonus: Get someone (or an entire community of someones) to review your cover, title, and first chapter. Do they think it's amazing? If not, what can you tweak before launch?

Exercise #7- This one is a two parter with no bonus. Take both these actions. Go to Amazon and experiment with searchable keywords until you find a list of search terms you can use that would lead readers to books like yours. Write down the list.

Browse the Amazon subcategories you want to be in until you're certain you've identified all of them. Go to KDP's help page (found in your KDP dashboard on the upper right) to see the list of what keywords you need to use in order to be in those categories.

Exercise #8- Brainstorm a reader magnet. Is there a narrative question you could answer with a short story? Something readers will love? If not, can you give them a character sheet, fan artwork, or something else relevant to them?

Bonus: Actually create that reader magnet.

Exercise #9- Finalize your book launch plan. What emails are you sending out and when? Are you posting on any forums? Write down every thing you're doing during launch week, and schedule it meticulously. This will make it simple to run your launch.

Exercise #10- Go to Amazon and look at the category or categories matching your book. Search the top 20 and look at the release date for each. Can you find any books that are selling a ton of copies more than a year after release? Write down those books.

These will become the case studies you use to position your own book for long term success.

Figure out what they're doing, and do as much of the same as is reasonably possible.

Bonus: Subscribe to the authors of these books via their author pages on Amazon. Each time you receive a release email from them, go back to the OLD book and see how well it's doing.

Exercise #11- Build your lead page, either using the tools offered by your mailing list provider, or by setting up a lead page account.

Bonus: Before setting up your lead page check out the signups for five of your favorite authors. What elements do they use? Can you use similar elements?

Exercise #12- Log into your website and check your metrics. How many people have clicked an Amazon link this month? How could you optimize your site to increase that? Is another author in your genre doing a great job there? What can you mine from their page to improve yours?

Exercise #13- Create or update your first autoresponder sequence. Are you sending a welcome email? How about checking in with fans? Add at least one email to the sequence.

Bonus: Tell your readers about your ARC program, and see how many are willing to join. Use this team to launch your next book.

Exercise #14- This may be the hardest exercise in the book, especially for newer authors. Find a mentee. This should be an author with less experience than you. Maybe it's a friend who writes, but isn't sure how to get to the next level. Offer them encouragement, and help them find the resources they need to get where you are.